Life Long Ago

by Janine Scott

Content and Reading Adviser: Mary Beth Fletcher, Ed.D.
Educational Consultant/Reading Specialist
The Carroll School, Lincoln, Massachusetts

Spyglass BOOKS

COMPASS POINT BOOKS

Minneapolis, Minnesota

Compass Point Books
3722 West 50th Street, #115
Minneapolis, MN 55410

Visit Compass Point Books on the Internet at *www.compasspointbooks.com*
or e-mail your request to *custserv@compasspointbooks.com*

Photographs ©: Minnesota Historical Society, cover, 8, 9, 10, 11, 13, 14, 18; Stock Montage, 4, 5, 21;
Bettmann/Corbis, 6, 7, 17, 19; Hulton Archive by Getty Images, 15.

Project Manager: Rebecca Weber McEwen
Editor: Heidi Schoof
Photo Selectors: Rebecca Weber McEwen and Heidi Schoof
Designer: Erin Scott, SARIN creative

Library of Congress Cataloging-in-Publication Data

Scott, Janine.
  Life long ago / by Janine Scott.
     p. cm. — (Spyglass books)
Summary: Takes a look at life one hundred years ago, compared
to life today.
Includes bibliographical references and index.
  ISBN 0-7565-0361-2 (hardcover)
  1. United States—Social life and customs—1865-1918—Juvenile
literature. [1. United States—Social life and customs—1865-1918.]
  I. Title. II. Series.
  E168 .S418 2002
  973.91'1—dc21
                              2002002737

Contents

Now and Then

One hundred years ago, there were cars, airplanes, telephones, radios, and schools. However, these were different from what we have today.

All Dressed Up

Women and girls wore long dresses, gloves, and hats—even on hot days. Men and boys wore *wool* suits, shirts with high collars, and hats.

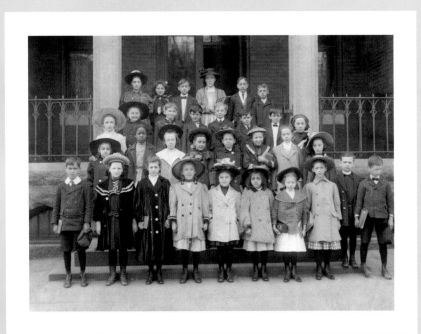

Wealthy people wore different clothes for each different activity they did during the day.

Work at Home

For people with a lot of
money, *electricity* changed
life in the home. Things
such as electric irons
made work easier to do.

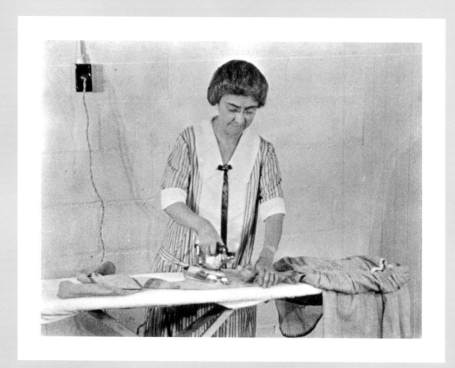

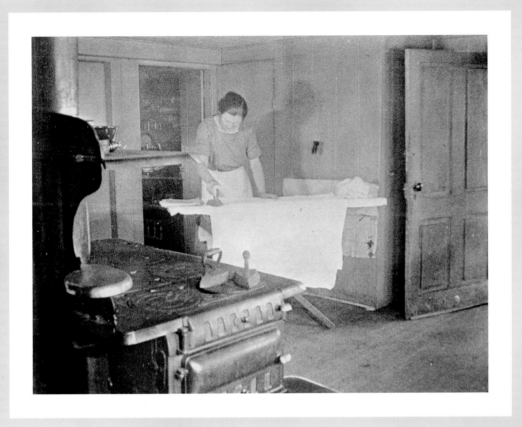

Most people heated heavy irons
over the fire and then pushed
the wrinkles out of clothes.

Daily Bread

People did not have refrigerators one hundred years ago. Instead, they bought their food nearly every day at grocery stores or markets.

Sometimes, ice and foods such as meat, vegetables, and milk were delivered to people's homes.

Let's Play

One hundred years ago, children had many *chores* to do. They played when they were done with their work.

Children played with *hoops*, yo-yos, marbles, and spinning tops.

Passing the Time

When people had free time, they found ways to enjoy themselves. Swimming was fun, even in heavy wool swimming suits.

People listened to *gramophones* at home and at school.

School Days

Children in the 1900s
spent much of their day
in school.

In some small towns,
children all went to
a one-room schoolhouse.

Children learned the "Three Rs": reading, writing, and arithmetic.

A Flying Start

In 1903, people built
the first airplane. In just
a few years, many people
were flying in airplanes.

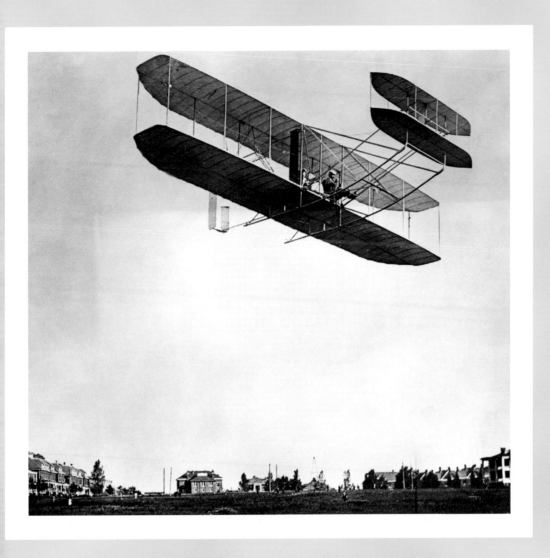

The Wright brothers invented the
first airplane that really flew.

Come for a Ride

Companies started making cars in 1901. Soon, many people had cars.

They could travel long distances faster and more easily than ever before.

The GREAT ARROW

Glossary

chore–a job around the house that people do regularly

electricity–a kind of energy that helps make things work, such as lightbulbs

hoop–a ring made of wood or metal that is rolled with a stick

gramophone–an early machine that played music on flat, round pieces of plastic or vinyl called records

wealthy–when someone has a lot of money

wool–fabric made from the hair of sheep

Learn More

Books

Hurdman, Charlotte. *Step into the Stone Age*. New York: Lorenz Books, 1998.

Smith, Nigel. *Then & Now Transportation*. Illustrated by Rob Shone and Graham White. Brookfield, Conn.: Copper Beech Books, 1997.

Weber, Valerie, and Jeraldine Jackson. *Food in Grandma's Day*. Minneapolis, Minn.: Carolrhoda Books, 1999.

Web Sites

www.sos.state.mi.us/history/ museum/musefaye/kidsatfa.html

kidshistory.tripod.com

Index

GR: G
Word Count: 193

From Janine Scott

I live in New Zealand, and have
two daughters. They love to read
books that are full of fun facts
and features. I hope you do, too!